MAJOR LEAGUE SPORTS

LAS LIGAS MAYORES

MLB
LA MLB

A Crabtree Branches Book

Un libro de Las Ramas de Crabtree

B. Keith Davidson

Translated by / Traducción de Santiago Ochoa

Crabtree Publishing

crabtreebooks.com

School-to-Home Support for Caregivers and Teachers

This high-interest book is designed to motivate striving students with engaging topics while building fluency, vocabulary, and an interest in reading. Here are a few questions and activities to help the reader build upon his or her comprehension skills.

Before Reading:

- *What do I think this book is about?*
- *What do I know about this topic?*
- *What do I want to learn about this topic?*
- *Why am I reading this book?*

During Reading:

- *I wonder why...*
- *I'm curious to know...*
- *How is this like something I already know?*
- *What have I learned so far?*

After Reading:

- *What was the author trying to teach me?*
- *What are some details?*
- *How did the photographs and captions help me understand more?*
- *Read the book again and look for the vocabulary words.*
- *What questions do I still have?*

Extension Activities:

- *What was your favorite part of the book? Write a paragraph on it.*
- *Draw a picture of your favorite thing you learned from the book.*

Apoyos de la escuela a los hogares para cuidadores y maestros

Este libro de gran interés está diseñado con temas atractivos para motivar a los estudiantes, a la vez que fomenta la fluidez, el vocabulario y el interés por la lectura. Las siguientes son algunas preguntas y actividades que ayudarán al lector a desarrollar sus habilidades de comprensión.

Antes de leer:

- *¿De qué creo que trata este libro?*
- *¿Qué sé sobre este tema?*
- *¿Qué quiero aprender sobre este tema?*
- *¿Por qué estoy leyendo este libro?*

Durante la lectura:

- *Me pregunto por qué...*
- *Tengo curiosidad por saber...*
- *¿En qué se parece esto a algo que ya conozco?*
- *¿Qué he aprendido hasta ahora?*

Después de la lectura:

- *¿Qué intentaba enseñarme el autor?*
- *¿Qué detalles recuerdo?*
- *¿Cómo me han ayudado las fotografías y los pies de foto a comprender mejor el libro?*
- *Vuelvo a leer el libro y busco las palabras del vocabulario.*
- *¿Qué preguntas me quedan?*

Actividades de extensión:

- *¿Cuál fue tu parte favorita del libro? Escribe un párrafo al respecto.*
- *Haz un dibujo de lo que más te gustó del libro.*

TABLE OF CONTENTS

ÍNDICE

BASEBALL BEGINNINGS

LOS INICIOS DEL BÉISBOL

Baseball was developed from the British bat-and-ball games of rounders, stoolball, and tut-ball. The rules as we know them didn't start to take shape until the 1830s. The first baseball game was played on June 4, 1838, in Ontario, Canada.

El béisbol se desarrolló a partir de juegos de pelota británicos como el *rounders*, el *stoolball* y el *tut-ball*. Las reglas, tal y como las conocemos, no comenzaron a tomar forma hasta la década de 1830. El primer partido de béisbol se jugó el 4 de junio de 1838 en Ontario, Canadá.

FUN FACT

The lowest attendance at a baseball game? The Florida Marlins set the record in 2011 with 347 fans showing up to see them play against the Cincinnati Reds. They blame Hurricane Irene, but the record stands.

UN DATO DIVERTIDO

¿Cuál ha sido la menor asistencia a un partido de béisbol? Los Marlins de Florida establecieron el récord en 2011, cuando solo 347 aficionados fueron a verlos jugar contra los Cincinnati Reds. La culpa la tuvo el huracán Irene, pero el récord se mantiene.

AS AMERICAN AS APPLE PIE

TAN ESTADOUNIDENSE COMO LA TARTA DE MANZANA

After that Ontario game, Americans took over. Alexander Cartwright created the first rulebook—the Knickerbocker Rules—and baseball became America's game. Since then the game has spread around the world with leagues all through Asia, Europe, and Latin America.

Después de ese partido en Ontario, los estadounidenses tomaron el control. Alexander Cartwright creó el primer reglamento (las Reglas Knickerbocker) y el béisbol se convirtió en el juego estadounidense por excelencia. Desde entonces el juego se ha extendido por todo el mundo, con ligas en Asia, Europa y América Latina.

William Rufus Wheaton was the first vice president of the Knickerbocker Base Ball Club.

William Rufus Wheaton fue el primer vicepresidente del Knickerbocker Baseball Club.

Knickerbocker Base Ball Club in 1847

El Knickerbocker Baseball Club en 1847.

Knickerbocker Club

El Knickerbocker Club

FUN FACT

The Knickerbocker Base Ball Club was the first organized baseball club.

UN DATO DIVERTIDO

El Knickerbocker Baseball Club fue el primer club de béisbol organizado.

ON THE MOUND
EN EL MONTÍCULO

Whether he throws a slider, a curve, or just a regular old fastball, the pitcher has to get the ball over the plate AND inside the batter's strike zone. If four balls are pitched outside the strike zone, the batter gets a walk.

Ya sea que lance una *slider*, una curva o una bola rápida tradicional, el lanzador tiene que hacer que la bola llegue arriba del plato del bateador, y dentro de la zona de *strike* del bateador. Si se lanzan cuatro pelotas fuera de la zona de strike, el bateador recibe un base por bola.

A pitcher rubs mud on the baseball to get the proper grip, but not just any mud. Jim Bintliff found the mud and only he knows where to get it.

Un lanzador frota barro en la pelota de béisbol para lograr el agarre adecuado, pero no es cualquier barro. Jim Bintliff encontró el barro y solo él sabe dónde conseguirlo.

pitcher's mound

montículo del lanzador

BEHIND THE PLATE
DETRÁS DEL PLATO

The catcher crouches behind home plate and has a great view of the infield. From here he can help the pitcher decide which style of pitch to use and also be on the lookout for runners trying to steal a base.

El receptor se pone en cuclillas detrás de la base del bateador y tiene una gran vista del campo interior. Desde allí puede ayudar al lanzador a decidir qué estilo de lanzamiento usar, además de estar atento a los corredores que intentan robar una base.

The catcher receiving a pitch.

El receptor recibe un lanzamiento.

The catcher is watching second base. He will throw the ball to stop the other team's player from stealing second base.

El receptor está de pie para ponchar a un corredor en segunda, antes de que robe una base.

FUN FACT

The average baseball game uses 60-70 baseballs. In Major League Baseball, a ball's life is about six pitches.

UN DATO DIVERTIDO

En un partido de béisbol promedio se utilizan entre 60 y 70 bolas de béisbol. En las Grandes Ligas, una bola dura apenas unos seis lanzamientos.

ON BASE
EN LA BASE

Each base is guarded by a baseman. Unlike the pitcher and the catcher, a baseman does not have to stay in his position. He runs to the high-action areas when fielding the ball.

Cada base está custodiada por un jugador de base. A diferencia del lanzador y del receptor, un jugador de base no tiene que permanecer en su posición: corre hacia las zonas de mayor acción cuando fildea la bola.

A baseman waits for the ball as a runner slides to base.

Un jugador de base espera la pelota mientras un corredor se desliza a la base.

THE SHORTSTOP

EL PARADOR EN CORTO

Standing between second and third bases, the shortstop position fields more balls than any other player on the diamond. A good shortstop is quick, agile, and has an accurate throwing arm to get the ball to first base when it's needed.

Situado entre la segunda y la tercera base, el parador en corto es el jugador que más pelotas lanza en el diamante. Un buen parador en corto es rápido, ágil y capaz de hacer lanzamientos precisos para que la pelota llegue a la primera base cuando más se necesita.

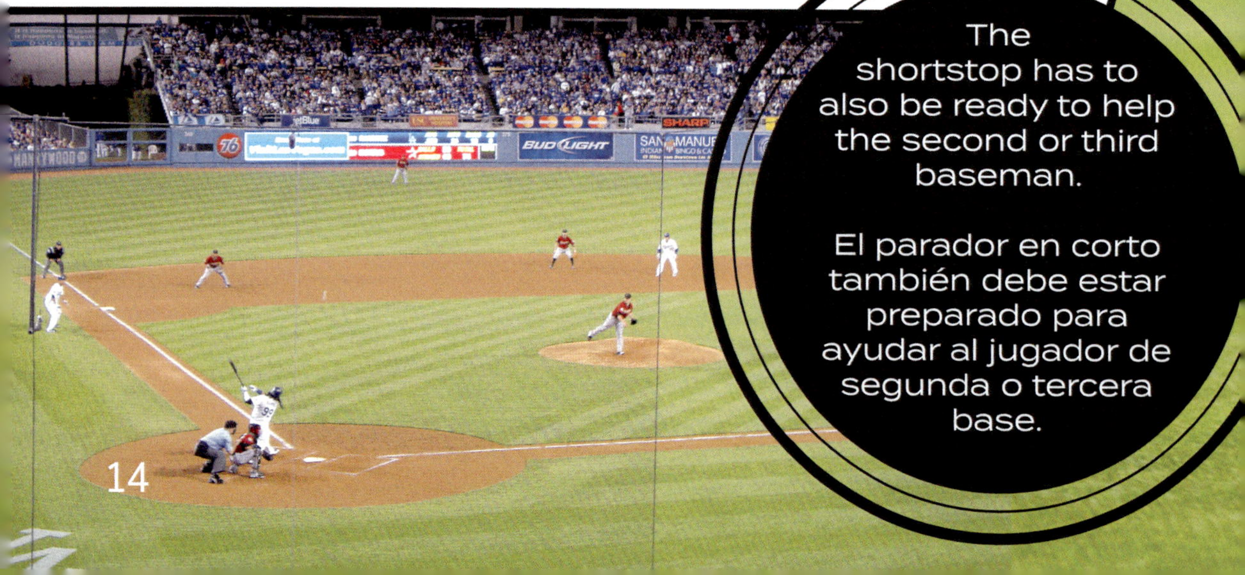

The shortstop has to also be ready to help the second or third baseman.

El parador en corto también debe estar preparado para ayudar al jugador de segunda o tercera base.

During the 2000 season, Derek Jeter, playing for the New York Yankees, became the only player to win both the All-Star game MVP and the World Series **MVP** in the same year.

Durante la temporada del 2000, Derek Jeter, que jugaba para los Yankees de Nueva York, se convirtió en el único jugador en ganar en un mismo año el **MVP** del partido de las estrellas y el MVP de la Serie Mundial.

OUTFIELD
EN EL JARDÍN

Chasing fly balls behind the bases, the three outfielders have a lot of turf to cover. One of the most exciting plays in baseball? When an outfielder runs to the back wall and jumps up to make a spectacular catch.

Al perseguir pelotas voladoras detrás de las bases, los tres jardineros tienen mucho terreno que cubrir. ¿Cuál es una de las jugadas más emocionantes del béisbol? Cuando un jardinero corre hacia la pared trasera y salta para hacer una atrapada espectacular.

FUN FACT

The Golden Glove is awarded every year to the best defensive player in each position. Pitcher Greg Maddux has the most with 18.

UN DATO DIVERTIDO

El Guante de Oro se concede cada año al mejor jugador defensivo en cada posición. El lanzador Greg Maddux, con 18 guantes, es el que más ha recibido.

Aaron Rowand reaches out to catch a fly ball.

Aaron Rowand se estira para atrapar una pelota voladora.

Barry Bonds

Barry Bonds holds the record for the most career home runs with 762.

Barry Bonds tiene el récord de más jonrones, con 762.

SWINGING FOR THE FENCES

ENVIÁNDOLA A LAS CERCAS

The batter tries to hit the ball over the outfield fence and score a home run, but there are many other types of hits. Grounders, line drives, bunts, and fly balls are all fair hits, as long as the ball doesn't go past the foul lines.

El bateador intenta golpear la pelota por encima de la valla del campo y hacer un jonrón, pero hay muchos otros tipos de bateo. Los rebotes, los lanzamientos de línea, los toques de bola y las pelotas voladoras son todos golpes válidos, siempre y cuando la pelota no sobrepase las líneas de *foul*.

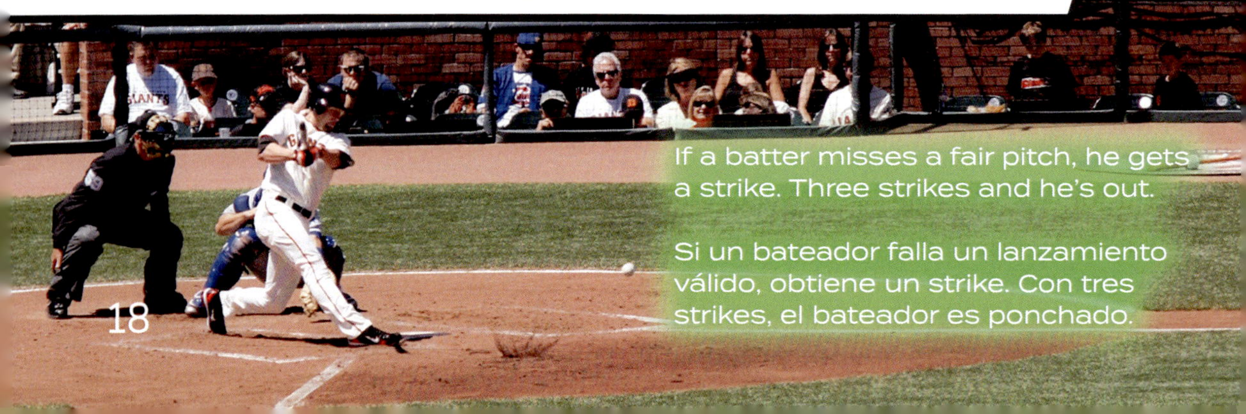

If a batter misses a fair pitch, he gets a strike. Three strikes and he's out.

Si un bateador falla un lanzamiento válido, obtiene un strike. Con tres strikes, el bateador es ponchado.

Javier Báez, shortstop for the Chicago Cubs

Javier Báez, parador en corto de los Cachorros de Chicago.

Mickey Mantle holds the record for the most World Series home runs with 18.

Mickey Mantle tiene el récord de más jonrones en una Serie Mundial, con 18.

UMPIRES
LOS AMPÁYER

Four umpires are used in an **MLB** game. Behind the plate, an umpire calls the balls, strikes, and fouls. That umpire is also in charge of calling runners safe at the plate. The base umpires determine whether a runner is safe or out at the bases.

En un partido de la **MLB** trabajan cuatro árbitros o ampáyer. Detrás del plato, un árbitro canta las bolas, los strikes y las faltas. Ese árbitro también está a cargo de decidir si un beisbolista hace una carrera o no. Los árbitros de base determinan si un corredor está *safe* en las bases o queda ponchado.

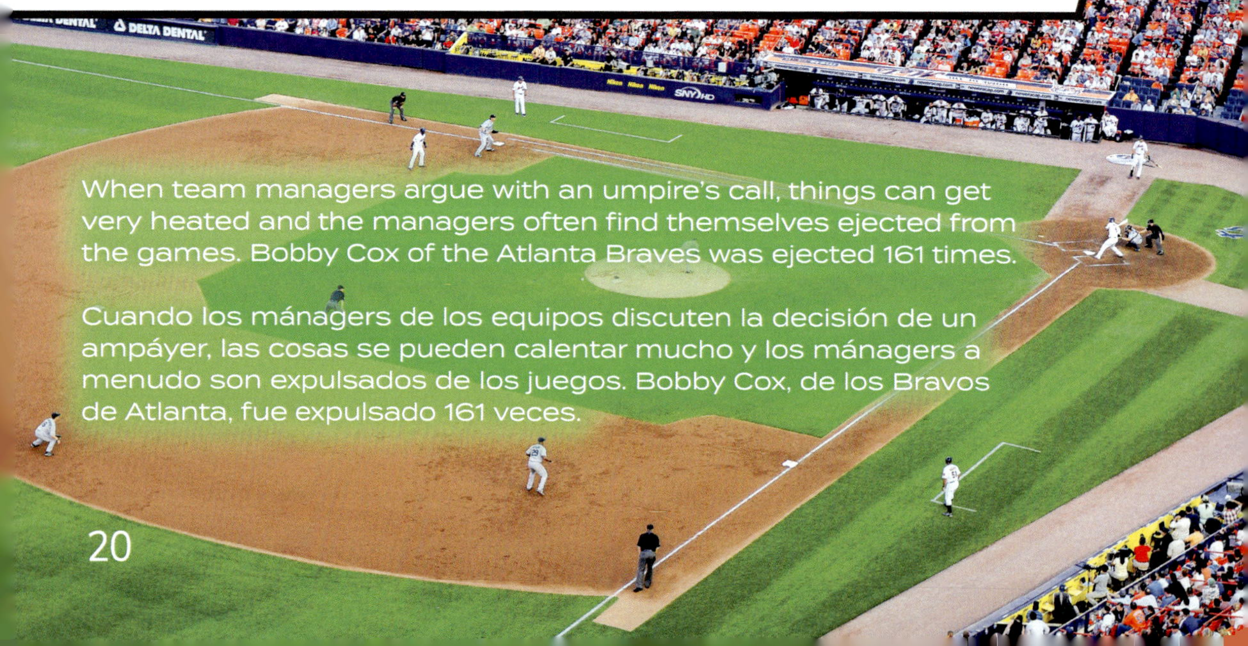

When team managers argue with an umpire's call, things can get very heated and the managers often find themselves ejected from the games. Bobby Cox of the Atlanta Braves was ejected 161 times.

Cuando los mánagers de los equipos discuten la decisión de un ampáyer, las cosas se pueden calentar mucho y los mánagers a menudo son expulsados de los juegos. Bobby Cox, de los Bravos de Atlanta, fue expulsado 161 veces.

19
PUJOLS
5

25

THE WORLD SERIES

LA SERIE MUNDIAL

An MLB season has 162 games. The season ends with the World Series, a series of seven games between the winners from the NL and the winners from the AL. The first team to win four games gets the Commissioner's Trophy.

Una temporada de la MLB tiene 162 juegos. La temporada termina con la Serie Mundial, una serie de siete partidos entre los ganadores de la NL y los ganadores de la AL. El primer equipo en ganar cuatro partidos se lleva el Trofeo del Comisionado.

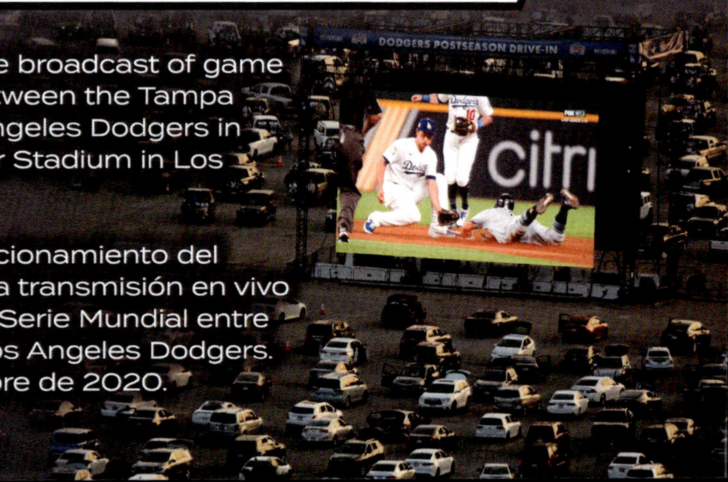

Fans watch a drive-in live broadcast of game 2 of the World Series between the Tampa Bay Rays and the Los Angeles Dodgers in the parking lot of Dodger Stadium in Los Angeles, Oct. 21, 2020.

Los fanáticos, en el estacionamiento del Dodger Stadium, ven una transmisión en vivo del segundo juego de la Serie Mundial entre los Tampa Bay Rays y Los Angeles Dodgers. Los Ángeles, 21 de octubre de 2020.

The Commissioner's Trophy is presented each year to the MLB team that wins the World Series.

El Trofeo del Comisionado se otorga cada año al equipo de la MLB que gana la Serie Mundial.

Yogi Berra has 10 World Series rings, the most by an individual player.

Yogi Berra tiene 10 anillos de la Serie Mundial, la mayor cantidad ganada por un solo jugador.

KEN GRIFFEY, JR.

CAREER 1989-2010
CARRERA DE 1989 A 2010

POSITION:
CENTER FIELDER
POSICIÓN:
JARDINERO CENTRAL

BATS BATEO	**LEFT IZQUIERDA**
THROWS LANZAMIENTOS	**LEFT IZQUIERDA**
HOME RUNS JONRONES	**630**
BATTING AVERAGE PROMEDIO DE BATEO	**.284**

JOSÉ BAUTISTA

CAREER **2004-2018**
CARRERA DE **2004 A 2018**

POSITION: **RIGHT FIELDER AND THIRD BASEMAN**
POSICIÓN: **JARDINERO DERECHO Y TERCERA BASE**

BATS *BATEO*	RIGHT DERECHA
THROWS *LANZAMIENTOS*	RIGHT DERECHA
HOME RUNS *JONRONES*	344
BATTING AVERAGE *PROMEDIO DE BATEO*	.247

NOLAN RYAN

CAREER **1966-1993**
CARRERA DE **1966 A 1993**

POSITION:
PITCHER
POSICIÓN:
LANZADOR

BATS ***BATEO***	**RIGHT** **DERECHA**
THROWS ***LANZAMIENTOS***	**RIGHT** **DERECHA**
STRIKEOUTS ***PONCHADOS***	**5,714**
WINS ***TRIUNFOS***	**324**

MIKE TROUT

CAREER 2011-PRESENT
CARRERA DE 2011 A LA FECHA

POSITION:
CENTER FIELDER
POSICIÓN:
JARDINERO CENTRAL

BATS ***BATEO***	**RIGHT** **DERECHA**
THROWS ***LANZAMIENTOS***	**RIGHT** **DERECHA**
HOME RUNS ***JONRONES***	**302**
BATTING AVERAGE ***PROMEDIO DE BATEO***	**.304**

THE MLB
LA MLB

Reaching the Major League is the dream of every young baseball player. It is the result of years of hard work and dedication. Start practicing now and maybe one day a kid will be reading an MLB book about you!

Llegar a las Grandes Ligas es el sueño de todo beisbolista joven. Es el resultado de años de trabajo duro y dedicación. Empieza a practicar ahora y tal vez algún día otro niño leerá sobre ti en un libro de la MLB.

FUN FACT

Deion Sanders played professional football AND baseball. He is the only person who has played in both the Super Bowl and the World Series. He's also the only person to hit a home run and score a touchdown in the same week.

UN DATO DIVERTIDO

Deion Sanders jugó fútbol americano y béisbol profesional. Es la única persona que ha jugado tanto en el Supertazón como en la Serie Mundial. Es también el único deportista que ha logrado batear un jonrón y anotar un touchdown en la misma semana.

Barry Larkin of the Cincinnati Reds

Barry Larkin, de los Rojos de Cincinnati.

GLOSSARY

AL (AY-EL): The American League of Professional Baseball Clubs that makes up half of the MLB

diamond (DYE-muhnd): The playing field used for baseball

fielding (FEEL-ding): Catching or stopping a ball that has been hit

fly balls (FLYE-ballz): Balls that have been hit high into the air

foul lines (FOWL LINEZ): The two lines running from home plate, through first base and third base, to the foul poles

MLB (EM-EL-BEE): Major League Baseball, an organization made up of two professional baseball leagues or groups: the American League (AL) and the National League (NL)

MVP (EM-VEE-PEE): Most Valuable Player

NL (EN-EL): The National League of Professional Baseball Clubs that makes up half of the MLB

outfielders (OUT-feel-derz): The three players that catch or stop the balls hit into the outfield

steal (STEEL): To move to a base without there being a batted ball or a walk

strike zone (STRIKE ZOHN): The area over home plate between the batter's knees and his shoulders

walk (WAWK): When a batter is awarded first base after the pitcher throws four pitches out of the strike zone, none of which are swung at by the hitter

GLOSARIO

AL: Liga Estadounidense de Clubes de Béisbol Profesional, compone la mitad de la MLB.

base por bola: Cuando un bateador obtiene la primera base después de que el lanzador hace cuatro lanzamientos fuera de la zona de strike, y en ninguno de los cuales el bateador ha intentado batear la bola.

diamante: El campo de juego utilizado para el béisbol.

fildea: Que atrapa o detiene una pelota que ha sido bateada.

jardineros: Los tres jugadores que atrapan o detienen las pelotas bateadas en los jardines.

líneas de *foul*: Las dos líneas que van desde el plato del bateador, pasan por la primera y la tercera base y llegan hasta los postes de *foul*.

MLB: Liga Mayor de Béisbol, una organización formada por dos ligas o grupos de béisbol profesional: la Liga Estadounidense (AL) y la Liga Nacional (NL).

MVP: El jugador más valioso.

NL: La Liga Nacional de Clubes de Béisbol Profesional, compone la mitad de la MLB.

pelotas voladoras: Pelota que ha sido golpeada hacia lo alto.

robar una base: Moverse a una base sin que haya una bola bateada o una base por bola.

zona de *strike*: El área entre las rodillas y los hombros del bateador, en la base.

INDEX

ÍNDICE ANALÍTICO

COOL FACTS:

Cy Young holds the record for most wins by a pitcher with 511, and also the most losses by a pitcher with 316.

Jackie Mitchell, at 17 years old, became the only woman to strike out both Babe Ruth and Lou Gherig.

The rarest pitch in baseball is called the screwball. It's a breaking ball that heads in the opposite direction of the pitcher's normal breaking ball.

DATOS CURIOSOS:

Con 511, Cy Young tiene el récord de más victorias de un lanzador. También el de más derrotas de un lanzador, con 316.

Jackie Mitchell, a los 17 años, se convirtió en la única mujer en ponchar a Babe Ruth y a Lou Gherig.

El lanzamiento más raro del béisbol se llama *screwball*. Se lanza doblando el brazo completamente en el sentido de las agujas del reloj para darle una rotación contraria a la natural.

WEBSITES FOR MORE COOL FACTS: SITIOS WEB CON MÁS DATOS CURIOSOS (PÁGINAS EN INGLÉS):

www.sikids.com/baseball

www.mlb.com/fans/kids/activities

https://kidskonnect.com/sports/baseball

ABOUT THE AUTHOR

B. Keith Davidson grew up playing with his three brothers and a host of neighborhood children, learning about life through sports and physical activity. He now teaches these games to his three children.

ACERCA DEL AUTOR

B. Keith Davidson creció jugando con sus tres hermanos y un montón de niños de su barrio; aprendió de la vida a través del deporte y la actividad física. Ahora enseña estos juegos a sus tres hijos.

Crabtree Publishing

crabtreebooks.com 800.387.7650

Written by/Escrito por: B. Keith Davidson
Designer/Diseñadora: Jennifer Dydyk
Editor/Editora: Tracy Nelson Maurer
Proofreader/Correctora de pruebas: Melissa Boyce
Translated by/Traducción de: Santiago Ochoa
Spanish-language copyediting and proofreading/ Maquetación y corrección en español: Base Tres
Coordinador de producción/Production manager: Candice Campbell

Hardcover 978-1-0398-6924-0
Paperback 978-1-0398-6903-5
Ebook (pdf) 978-1-0398-6945-5
Epub 978-1-0398-6966-0

Library and Archives Canada Cataloguing in Publication
Available at the Library and Archives Canada

Library of Congress Cataloging-in-Publication Data
Available at the Library of Congress

Printed in the U.S.A./Impreso en los Estados Unidos/CP112025

Published in Canada
Publicado en Canadá
Crabtree Publishing
616 Welland Avenue
St. Catharines, Ontario
L2M 5V6

Published in the United States
Publicado en los Estados Unidos
Crabtree Publishing
347 Fifth Avenue
Suite 1402-145
New York, NY 10016

Photographs/Fotografías: COVER: Top photo Shutterstock.com/ Vasyl Shulga, players © KYDPL KYODO/Associated Press, PG 5: ©shutterstock.com/Matt Trommer, PG 6: ©Wheaton_PD, PG 7: ©NYKnickerbockers_PD, PG 8: ©itstock.com/33ft, PG 9: ©Debby Wong / Shutterstock.com (top), ©Mark Herreid / Shutterstock.com, PG 10: ©Arturo Holmes / Shutterstock.com, PG 11: ©Arturo Holmes / Shutterstock.com, PG 12: ©Eric Broder Van Dyke | Dreamstime.com, PG 13: ©Arturo Holmes / Shutterstock.com (inset), ©JASON TENCH / Shutterstock.com (top), PG 14: ©Eric Broder Van Dyke / Shutterstock.com, PG 15: ©Sports Images| Dreamstime.com, PG 16: ©Eric Broder Van Dyke / Shutterstock.com, PG 17: © Sports Images| Dreamstime.com (inset), ©Eric Broder Van Dyke / Shutterstock.com, PG 18: ©Eric Broder Van Dyke| Dreamstime.com, PG 19: ©Keeton Gale / Shutterstock.com (top), ©MantlePortrait_PD, PG 20: ©Demerzel21| Dreamstime.com, PG 21: ©Lawrence Weslowski Jr| Dreamstime.com (inset), © Alexa Sklar| Dreamstime.com, PG 22: ©Ringo Chiu / Shutterstock.com, PG 23: ©Gopheliad| Dreamstime.com, ©Googie man_https://creativecommons.org/licenses/by-sa/3.0/deed.en, PG 24: ©Jerry Coli| Dreamstime.com, PG 25: ©Paul Mckinnon| Dreamstime.com, PG 26: ©Jerry Coli| Dreamstime.com, PG 27: ©Mike Trout © Keith Allison https://creativecommons.org/licenses/by-sa/2.0/deed.en, PG 28: ©DFree / Shutterstock.com, © Sports Images| Dreamstime.com (inset), PG 29: ©Sports Images | Dreamstime.com